THE LAND: THE PROMISE, GIFT, AND CHALLENGE OF THE LAND IN BIBLICAL FAITH

GOLU KUMAR

Contents

CHAPTER ONE

PART I.

Tell me how many pieces you have by telegraph.

The Steamship Company used this method to let the savvy agent know that it wanted to know how many Russian Jews were being smuggled into the steerage of one of their Atlantic liners from the Pale.

The astute agent's task was simple enough. The tales he told of America were only the clarification of a nebulous vision of the land flowing with milk and honey that hovered golden-rayed before all these hungry eyes. To the denizens of the Pale, in their cellars, in their gutter-streets, in their semi-subterranean shops consisting mainly of shutters and annihilating one another's profits; to the congested populations newly reinforced by the driving back of thousands from beyond the Pale, and yet multiplying still by an improvident reliance on Providence; to the old people pauperized by the removal of the vodka business to Christian hands, and the young people dammed back from their natural outlets by Pan-Slavic ukases, and clogged with whimsical edicts and rescripts--the astute agent's offer of getting you through Germany, without even a Russian passport, by a simple passage from Libau to New York, was peculiarly alluring.

It was almost an over-baiting of the hook on the part of the too astute agent to whisper that he had had secret information of a new thunderbolt about to be launched at the Pale; whereby the period of service for Jewish conscripts would be extended to fifteen years, and the area of service would be extended to Siberia.

He responded by sending a telegraph that read, "377 pieces."

He offered other business he might secure for the line in a letter.

The Company wrote cautiously, "Confine yourselves to freight," for even in sealed envelopes, one cannot be too cautious. More is always better.

Freight! The word was accurate. Did not even government records mention how these Muzhik exploiters were often crammed into their hovels like salt herrings in a barrel and slept in sites that were tallow or leather workshops during the day?

Therefore, it seemed only logical to be transported as cargo. Nevertheless, because they were all made of human beings, each of these "parts" had a past; one of those pasts is described here.

PART II.

The weavers‘ colony, where Srul got engaged to Biela, was the poorest place in the Pale, by far. The dowries, which had been known to ignite the hearts of so many young men, had reached their lowest point, and Biela, even if she didn't have a good chance of getting married, could take comfort in the fact that she was romantically loved.

Even the attraction of _kest_--temporary maintenance of the young couple by the father-in-law--was wanting in Biela's case, for the simple reason that she had no father, both her parents having died of the effort to get a living. For marriage portion and _kest_, Biela could only bring her dark beauty, and even that was perhaps less than it seemed. For you scarcely ever saw Biela apart from her homely quasi-mother, her elder sister Leah, who, like the original Leah, had "tender eyes," which combined with a pock-marked face to ensure her premature recognition as an old maid. The inflamed eyelids were the only legacy Leah's father had left her.

From Saul's side, though his parents were living, came even fainter hope of the wedding canopy. Saul's father was blind--perhaps further evidence that the local hygienic conditions were nocuous to the eye in particular--and Srul himself, who had occupied most of his time in learning to weave Rabbinic webs, had only just turned his attention to cloth, though Heaven was doubtless pleased with the gear of _Gemara_ he had gathered in his short sixteen years. The old weaver had--in more than one sense--seen better days before his affliction and the great factories came on: days when the independent hand-weaver might sit busily before the loom from the raw dawn to the black midnight, taking his meals at the bench; days when, moreover, the "piece" of satin-faced cloth was many ells shorter. "But they make up for the extra length," he would say with pathetic humor, "by cutting the pay shorter."

The same sense of humor enabled him to bear up against the forced rests that increasing slackness brought the hand-weavers, while the factories whirred on. "Now is the proverb fulfilled," he cried to his unsmiling wife, "for there are two Sabbaths a week." Alas! as the winter grew older and colder, it became a week of Sabbaths. The wheels stood still; in all the colony not a spool was reeled. It was unprecedented. Gradually the factories had stolen the customers. Some sat waiting dazedly for the raw yarns they knew could no longer come at this season; others left the suburb in which the colony had drowsed from time immemorial, and sought odd jobs in the town, in the frowning shadows of the factories. But none would enter the factories themselves, though these were ready to suck them in on one sole condition.

Ah! here was the irony of the tragedy. The one condition was the one condition the poor weavers could not accept. It was open to them to reduce the week of Sabbaths to its ancient and diurnal dimensions, provided the Sabbath itself came on Sunday. Nay, even the working day offered them was less, and the wage was more than their own. The deeper irony within this irony was that the proprietor of every one of these factories was a brother in Israel! Jeshurun grew fat and kicking.

Even the old blind man's composure deserted him when it began to be borne in on his darkness that the younger weavers meditated surrender. The latent explosives generated through the years by their perusal of un-Jewish books in insidious "Yiddish" versions, now bade fair to be touched to eruption by this paraded prosperity of wickedness; wickedness that had even discarded the caftan and shaved the corners of its beard.

However, you, the apple of my eye, would sooner die than violate the Sabbath, right?

"Father," said the young man, "I have been young and now I am old, but never have I saw the upright forsaken, nor his seed begging for bread." The young man's voice quivered at the very notion.

"My boy! An actual ember from the Patriarchs! Then the old guy hugged the youngster close to him and kissed him on the pious cheeks where the boy's earlocks dangled.

His mother, who couldn't get her mind off her grandchildren, added, "But if Biela did persuade thee so that thou mightst have the wherewithal to marry her."

I won't join your service, mum, not for apples of gold.

"Mother, I won't join the service of these serpents for apples of gold."

The mother mumbled, "Biela is fair to sight, though, and thou art getting on in years.

The old man assured them, "Leah would not give Biela to a Sabbath-breaker."

Yes, but what if she delivers her to a wage earner? the mother persisted. Remember that Biela is only a year younger than you and has already turned fifteen.

But Leah kept firm to the truth she had plighted on behalf of Biela, even though the young man's family sank lower and lower, till it was at last reduced from the little suburban wooden cottage, with the spacious courtyard, to one corner of a large town-cellar, whose population became amphibious when the Vistula overflowed.

Even when his father's heart stopped beating, Srul remained steadfast in the path Israel had chosen with the Sabbath bride and could not be moved. Perhaps because he was spared the sight of his malnourished fellow troglodytes, the elderly guy remained the cellar's cheeriest inhabitant till the very end. He gave the cellar the name "Arba Kanfôs" after the four-cornered fringed gown he wore, and he occasionally claimed that these were the "Four Corners" from whence God would gather Israel, according to the Prophets.

PART III.

An agent is seldom required to be smart in such a situation.

There were "pieces" available for the taking. The fact that they weren't made of gold was their only drawback. The idle weavers were unable to pay for their travel expenses, let alone the agent's fee for getting them through illegally.

Soul lamented to Leah, "I might get to a land where there is labor without breaking the Sabbath, a land to which Biela could accompany me as I waxed in substance if I only had a few hundred roubles."

Leah supported her household of three--for there was a younger sister, Tsirrélé, who, being only nine, did not count except at meal times--on the price of her piece-work at the Christian umbrella factory, where, by a considerate Russian law, she could work on Sunday, though the Christians might not. Thus she earned, by literal sweating in a torrid atmosphere, three roubles, all except a varying number of kopecks, every week. And when you live largely on black bread and coffee, you may, in years, save a good deal, even if you have three mouths. Therefore, Leah had the sum that Srul mentioned so wistfully, put by for a rainy day (when there should be no umbrellas to make). And as the sum had kept increasing, the notion that it might form the nucleus of an establishment for Biela and Srul had grown clearer and clearer in her mind, which it tickled delightfully. But the idea that now came to her of staking all on a possible future was agitating.

She hesitantly answered, "We might, perhaps, be able to cobble together the money. "But—" The Russian saying entered her mouth as she shook her head. "The dew may kill you before the sun rises."

Soul quickly began to reiterate the agent's guarantees. And there in front of their eyes, in the Land of Promise, the wedding canopy rose majestically, and Biela's figure flitted by while wearing the bridal wreath.

What will happen to your mother, though? Leah queried.

The soap bubbles of Srul burst. He temporarily lost sight of the fact that he had a mother.

Upon noticing his overcast look, Leah hastened to say, "She might come to live with us.

"That would be an excessive load, I see. Tsirrélé is developing as well."

Leah added, smiling, "Tsirrélé eats quite as much now as she will in ten years," as she thought affectionately of her beloved, adorable child, her gay whims, and quirky caprices.

And my mother doesn't eat much," Srul replied hesitantly.

Soul was thus reduced to a "piece" and dropped into the Land of Promise.

PART IV.

The movements of the particular component, Srul, were the main focus of existence for the four females who were left behind—weird pieces of two families thrown into an even stranger one. The three-roomed wooden cottage's inhabitants quickly settled into a routine, with Leah going to the tropical factory every day, Biela cleaning the house while daydreaming of her lover, little Tsirrélé running around and chattering like the squirrel she was, and Srul's mother nodding off while giving criticism and pining for her late son and her unborn grandchildren. When Srul's first letter from the Land of Promise with its intriguing graphic stamp arrived, it appeared that this had always been the foundation of the home.

"I had a lucky escape, God is thanked," Srul wrote. "For when I arrived in New York I had only fifty-one roubles in my pocket. Now it seems that these rich Americans are so afraid of being overloaded with paupers that they will not let you in if you have less than fifty dollars unless you can prove you are sure to prosper. And a dollar, my dear Biela, is a good deal more than a rouble. However, blessed be the Highest One, I learned of this ukase just the day before we arrived, and was able to borrow the difference from a fellow passenger, who lent me the money to show the Commissioners. Of course, I had to give it back as soon as I was passed, and as I had to pay him five roubles for the use of it, I set foot on the soil of freedom with only forty-six. However, it was well worth it; for just think, beloved Biela, if I had been shipped back and all that money wasted! The interpreter also said to me, 'I suppose you have got some work to do here?' 'I wish I had,' I said. No sooner had the truth slipped out than my heart seemed turned to ice, for I feared they would reject me after all as a poor wretch out of work. But quite the contrary; it seemed this was only a trap, a snare of the fowler. Poor Kaminski fell into it--you remember the red-haired weaver who sold his looms to the Maggid's brother-in-law. He said he had agreed to take a place in a glove factory. It is true, you know, that some Polish Jews have made a glove town in the north, so the poor man thought that would sound plausible. Hence you may expect to see Caminski's red hair back again unless he takes ship again from Libau and tells the truth at the second attempt. I left him howling in a wooden pen, and declaring he would kill himself rather than face his friends at home with the brand on his head of not being good enough for America. He did not understand that contract laborer are not let in. Protection is the word they call it. Hence, I thank God that my father--his memory for a blessing!--taught me to make Truth the law of my mouth, as it is written. Verily was the word of the Talmud (Tractate Sabbath) fulfilled at the landing stage: 'Falsehood cannot stay, but the truth remains forever.' With God's help, I shall remain here all my life, for it is a land overflowing with milk and honey. I had almost forgotten to tell my dove that the voyage was hard and bitter as the Egyptian bondage; not because of the ocean, over which I passed as easily as our forefathers over the Red Sea, but because of the harshness of the overseers, who regarded not our complaints that the meat was not _kosher_, as promised by the agent. Also, the butter and meat plates were mixed up. I and many with me lived on dry bread, nor could we always get hot water to make coffee. When my Biela comes across the great waters--God send her soon--she must take with her salt meat of her own."

From the first, Srul courageously assumed that the meat would soon have to be packed; nay, that Leah might almost set about salting it at once. Even the slow beginnings of his profits as a peddler did not daunt him. "A great country," he wrote on paper stamped with the Stars and Stripes, with an eagle screaming on the envelope. "No special taxes for the Jews, permission to travel where you please, the schools open freely to our children, no passports and papers at every step, above all, no conscription. No wonder the people call it God's own country. Truly, as it is written, this is none other but the House of God, this is the Gate of Heaven. And when Biela comes, it will be Heaven." Letters like this enlarged the little cottage as with an American room, brightened it as with a fresh wash of blue paint. Despite the dreary grind of the week, Sabbaths and festivals found the household joyous enough. The wedding canopy of Srul and Biela was a beacon of light for all four, which made life livable as they struggled toward it. Nevertheless, it came but slowly to meet them: nearly three years oozed by before Srul began to lift his eye toward a store. The hereditary weaver of business combinations had emerged tardily from beneath the logic-weaver and the cloth-weaver, but of late he had been finding himself. "If I could only get together five hundred dollars clear," he wrote to Leah. "For that is all I should have to pay down for a ladies' store near Broadway, and just at the foot of the stairs of the Elevated Railway. What a pity I have only four hundred and thirty-five dollars! Stock and goodwill, and only five hundred dollars cash! The other five hundred could stand over at five percent. If I were once in the store I could gradually get some of the rooms above (there is already a parlor, in which I shall sleep), and then, as soon as I was making a regular profit, I could send Biela and mother their passage-money, and my wife could help 'the boss' behind the counter."

Leah paid 35 roubles to speed up the happy day, and soon enough, Srul was in possession and a picture of the actual business appeared to cheer their tired eyes and widen the neighbors'. Since Srul's peaked cap and caftan had been replaced with a blazer and a bowler, the portrait he had taken 18 months earlier was not appropriate for display. If not for the ear locks that were still there, he would have appeared to be a factory owner. In exchange, Leah put her arm around Biela's waist and Tsirrélé sat on his mother's lap in a picture of the four taken collectively for economic reasons.

PART V.

But the new "boss" still had a long, arduous battle ahead of him, and two years passed with their share of good fortune and bad, of deals and bad debts, are the imaginative marriage canopy (that seemed to cross the Atlantic) began to stand firmly on American soil. Before Srul delivered Biela the money for her trip and a dapper "waist" from his store for her to wear, the third year had barely ended. While Saul was still unable to withdraw his mother's fare from his capital, Biela was too afraid to travel alone.

Naturally, Leah offered to advance it, but Biela angrily declined since a new hope had started to emerge in her heart.

Why should she ever be cut off from her family? A few extra or fewer months would have made no difference as her marriage had been postponed for these five and a half years. So let Leah's savings go toward paying for her travel (as well as Tsirrélé's) and giving her a head start in the New World. She pleaded, "It rains even in America, and there are umbrella factories there. "You'll earn twice as much money. Observe Soul!"

And there was a new fear, too, which haunted Biela's aching heart, but which she dared not express to Leah. Leah's eyes were getting worse. The temperature of the factory was a daily hurt, and then, too, she had read so many vilely printed Yiddish books and papers by the light of the tallow candle. What if she were going blind? What if, while she, Biela, was happy with Srul, Leah should be starving with Tsirrélé? No, they must all remain together: and she clung to her sister, with tears.

To Leah, the prospect of witnessing her sister's happiness was so seductive that she tried to take the lowest estimate of her chances of finding work in New York. Her savings, almost eaten up by the journey, could not last long, and it would be terrible to have to come upon Saul for help, a man with a wife and (if God were good) children, to say nothing of his old mother. No, she could not risk Tsirrélé's bread.

But the increased trouble with her eyes turned her in favor of going, though, curiously enough, for a side reason quite unlike Biela's. Leah, too, was afraid of a serious breakdown, though she would not hint her fears to anyone else. From her miscellaneous Yiddish reading, she had gathered that miraculous eye doctors lived in Königsberg. Now a journey to Germany was not to be thought of; if she went to America, however, it could be taken en route. It would be a sort of saving, and few things appealed to Leah as much as the economy. This was why, some four months later, the ancient furniture of the blue-washed cottage was sold off, and the quartette set their faces for America by way of Germany. The farewell to the home of their youth took place in the cemetery among the high-shouldered Hebrew-speaking stones. Leah and Biela passionately invoked the spirits of their dead parents and bade them watch over their children. The old woman scribbled Srul and Biela's interlinked names over the flat tomb of a holy scholar. "Take their names up to the Highest One," she pleaded. "Entreat that their quiver is full, for the sake of thy righteousness."

More dead than alive, the four "pieces" with their bundles arrived at Hamburg. Days and nights of traveling packed like "freight" in hard, dirty wooden carriages, the endless worry of passports, tickets, questions, hygienic inspections and processes, the illegal exactions of petty officials, the strange phantasmagoria of places and faces--all this had left them dazed. Only two things kept up their spirits--the image of Srul waiting on the Transatlantic wharf in hymeneal attire, and the "pooh-pooh" of the miraculous Königsberg doctor, reassuring Leah as to her eyes. There was nothing radically the matter. Even the inflamed eyelids--though incurable, because hereditary--would improve with care. Peasant-like, Leah craved a lotion. "The sea voyage and the rest will do you more good than my medicines. And don't read so much." Not a groschen did Leah have to pay for the great specialist's services. It was the first time in her hard life anybody had done anything for her for nothing, and her involuntary weeping over this phenomenon tended to hurt the very eyelids under attention. They were still further taxed by the kindness of the Jewish committee at Hamburg, on the lookout to smooth the path of poor emigrants and overcome their dietary difficulties. But it was a crowded ship, and our party reverted again to "freight." With some of the other females, they were accommodated in hammocks swung over the very dining tables, so that they must needs rise at dawn and be cleared away before breakfast. The hot, oily whiff of the cooking engines came through the rocking doorway. Of the quartette, only Tsirrélé escaped sea-sickness, but "baby" was too accustomed to being petted and nursed to be able suddenly to pet and nurse, and she would spend hours on the slip of lower deck, peering into the fairy saloons which were vivified by bugle instead of a bell, and in which beautiful people ate dishes fit for the saints in Heaven. By an effort of will, Leah soon returned to her rôle of factotum, but the old woman and Biela remained limp to the end. Fortunately, there was only one day of heavy rolling and battened-down hatches. For the bulk of the voyage, the great vessel brushed the pack of waves disdainfully aside. And one wonderful day, amid unspeakable joy, New York arrived, preceded by a tug and by a boat that conveyed inquiring officials. The great statue of Liberty, on Bedloe's Island, upheld its torch to light the newcomers' path. Soul--there he is on the wharf, dear old Soul!--God bless him! despite his close-cropped hair and his shaven earlocks. Ah! Heaven is praised! Don't you see him waving? Ah, but we, too, must be content with waving. For here only the _tschinovniks_ of the gilded saloon may land. The "freight" must be packed later into rigid gangs, according to the ship's manifest, transferred to a smaller steamer, and discharged on Ellis Island, a little beyond Bedloe's.

PART VI.

Additionally, an unpredicted horrible event occurred at Ellis Island: a shipwreck in the very harbor.

The doctor thought Leah's eye problem was contagious as the "freight" moved slowly down the corridor cages in the large, empty hall, much like livestock being examined at ports by the veterinary surgeon.

He wrote down his diagnosis: "Granular lids — contagious." And this prognosis served as a fiery sword that guarded against Leah, the Land of Promise, in all directions.

"But it is not infectious," she protested in her best German. "It is only in the family."

"So I perceive," dryly replied America's Guardian Angel, who was now examining the obvious sister clinging to Leah's skirts. And in Biela, heavy-eyed with sickness and want of sleep, his suspicious vision easily discovered a reddish rim of the eyelid that lent itself to the same fatal diagnosis and sent her to join Leah in the dock of the rejected. The fresh-faced Tsirrélé and the wizen-faced mother of Srul passed unscrutinized, and even the dread clerk at the desk who asked questions was content with their oath that the wealthy Srul would support them. Saul was, indeed, sent for at once, as Tsirrélé was too pretty to be let out under the mere protection of a Polish crone.

When the full truth that neither she nor Biela was to set foot in New York burst through the daze in Leah's brain, her protest grew frantic.

"But my sister has nothing the matter with her--nothing. O _gnädiger Herr_, have pity. The Königsberg doctor--the great doctor--told me I had no disease, no disease at all. And even if I have, my sister's eyes are pure as the sunshine.

Look, _mein Herr_, look again. See," and she held up Biela's eyelids and passionately kissed the wet bewildered eyes. "She is to be married, my lamb--her bridegroom awaits her on the wharf. Send _me_ back, _gnädiger Herr_; I ought not to have come. But for God's sake, don't keep Biela out, don't." She wrung her hands. But the marriage card had been played too often in that hall of despairing dodges. "Oh, _Herr Doktor_," and she kissed the coat-tail of the ship's doctor, "plead for us; speak a word for her."

The ship's doctor spoke a word on his behalf. It was he who had endorsed the two girls' health certificates at Hamburg, and he would be blamed by the Steamship Company, which would have to ship the sisters back free, and even defray their expenses while in quarantine at the dépôt. He ridiculed the idea that the girls were suffering from anything contagious. But the native doctor frowned, immovable.

Leah grew hysteric. It was the first time in her life she had lost her sane standpoint. "Your eye is affected," she shrieked, her dark pock-marked face almost black with desperate anger, "if you cannot see that it is only because my sister has been weeping, because she is ill from the voyage. But she carries no infection--she is healthy as an ox, and her eye is the eye of an eagle!" She was ordered to be silent, but she shrieked angrily, "The German doctors know, but the Americans have no _Bildung_."

Biela wailed, wrapping her arms over Leah's panting breast, "Oh, don't, Leah." What's the point? However, the unstoppable Leah received a Special Inquiry ticket and demanded a hearing in the Commissioners' Court.

"Kindly let her in and send the other one back, fellas. Tsirrélé and I will return together. Regarding the infant, it makes no difference."

The nice folks sitting on the bench were very nice, but America needs to be safeguarded.

The interpreter assured her, "You can take the young one and the old one both back with you." However, they are the only people we can admit.

Leah and Biela were driven back among the damned. The favored twain stood helplessly in their happier compartment. Even Tsirrélé, the squirrel, was dazed. Presently the spruce Srul arrived--to find the expected raptures replaced by funereal misery. He wormed his way dizzily into the cage of the rejected. It was not the etiquette of the Pale to kiss one's betrothed bride, but Srul stared dully at Biela without even touching her hand, as if the Atlantic already rolled again between them. There was a pretty climax to the dreams of years!

Biela hesitated, "My poor Srul, we must return to Hamburg to be married."

"And close my shop?" Soul screamed. "The dollar is spinning here. We currently have what is known as a boom. No other land on the planet is like ours."

Leah was brought to her senses by the other people's desolation.

"Listen, Saul," she said hurriedly. "It is all my fault because I wanted to share in the happiness. I ought not to have come. If we had not been together they never would have suspected Biela's eyes--who would notice the little touch of inflammation which is the most she has ever suffered from? She shall come again in another ship, all alone--for she knows now how to travel. Is it not so, Biela, my lamb? I will see you on board, and Srul will meet you here, although not till you have passed the doctor so that no one will have a chance of remembering you. It will cost a heap, alas! but I can get some work in Hamburg, and the

Jews there have hearts of gold. Eh, Biela, my poor lamb?"

Yes, Leah, you can always counsel yourself. Biela caressed the pock-marked cheek of her sister while placing her damp face next to hers.

Soul enthusiastically agreed. Leah would be left alone in the Old World, but nobody at the time realized this. The issue of how to make the bride enter obstructed the entire horizon.

Saul replied, "Yes, yes." Tsirrélé's mother will take care of her, and Biela will move in less than three weeks.

Leah argued that three weeks was too soon. We need to hold out a little while longer till the doctor forgets.

Soul sighed, "But I've already waited for so long!

Tears of empathy streamed into Leah's eyes. "I should have avoided creating such a fuss. She will now stay in the physician's memory.

Leah's eyes filled with sympathetic tears. "I ought not to have made so much fuss. Now she will stick in the doctor's mind. Forgive me, dear Srul, I will do my best and try to make amends."

Leah and Biela were taken away to the hospital, where they remained isolated from the world till the steamer sailed back to Hamburg. Herein, generously lodged, they had ample leisure to review the situation. Biela discovered that the new plan would leave Leah deserted, Leah remembered that she would be deserting little Tsirrélé. Both agreed that Tsirrélé must go back with them, till they bethought themselves that her passage would have to be paid for, as she was not refused. And every kopeck was precious now. "Let the child stay till I get back," said Biela. "Then I will send her to you."

But though Saul and his mother and Tsirrélé got on board to see them off, and Tsirrélé gave graphic accounts of the wonders of the store and the rooms prepared for the bride, to say nothing of the great city itself, and Srul brought Biela and Leah splendid specimens of his stock for their adornment, yet it was a horrible thing for them to go back again without having once trodden the sidewalks of the Land of Promise. And when the others were tolled off, as by a funeral bell, and became specks in a swaying crowd; when the dock receded and the cheers and good-byes faded, and the waving handkerchiefs became a blur, and the Statue of Liberty dwindled, and the lone waste of waters faced them once more, Leah's optimism gave way, a chill sinister shadow fell across her new plan, some ominous intuition traversed her like a shudder, and she turned away lest Biela should see her tears.

PART VII.

This dejection was short-lived. Leah was not a hopeless person by nature. But when she returned to Hamburg and recounted her difficult situation to the excellent committee, one of the members gave her an informal hint that was like a flash of light from Heaven and was the committee's response to her persistent prayers. This exceeded even her highest expectations. There were other ways to get to the Land of Promise besides Ellis Island. They weren't as picky in Canada, so you could travel about there and sneak in by train from Montreal without drawing any attention. True, there was the additional cost.

Expense! Leah would have gladly parted with her last rouble to unite Biela with her bridegroom. There must be no delay. A steamer for Canada was waiting to sail. What a fool she had been not to think that out for herself! Yes, but there was Biela's timidity again to consider. Travel by herself through this unknown Canada! And then if they were not so particular, why could not Leah slip through likewise?

"Yes, but my eyes stand out more. I might hurt you farther now."

"At the landing stage and the border, we will split up. We'll act like total strangers." The crisis made Biela more astute.

Leah reasoned, "Well, I can only lose the passage money," and she decided to take the chance. She had just finished writing a letter to Srul outlining their audacious plot to invade New York by land when Biela said:

"Stupid Soul! And if I don't get in!" Leah's face dropped.

"True," she thought. He'll experience a heartbreaking disappointment that's worse than previously.

"Let's not raise their expectations. After all, if we get admitted, we won't be any later than when our letter was sent. then consider the delight of the unexpected."

"You're right, Biela," Leah said, and the anticipation of the surprise returned to her face.

The journey to Canada was longer than to the States, and the "freight" was less companionable. There were fewer Jews and women, more stalwart shepherds, miners, and dock laborers. When after eleven days, the land came, it was not touched, but only remained cheeringly on the horizon for the rest of the voyage. At last, the sisters found themselves unmolested on one of the many wharves of Montreal. But they would not linger a day in this unhomely city. The next morning saw them, dazed and worn out but happy-hearted, dodging the monstrous catapults of the New York motorcars, while a Polish porter helped them with their bundles and convoyed them toward Srul's store. Ah, what ecstasy to be unregarded units of this free chaotic crowd. Outside the store--what a wonderful store it was, larger than the largest in the weavers' colony!--the sisters paused a moment to roll the coming bliss under their tongues. They peeped in. Ah, there is Srul behind the counter, waiting for customers. Ah, ah, he little knows what customers are waiting for him! They turned and kissed each other for mere joy.

Leah chuckled, "Draw your shawl over your face." "Enter and inquire if he is wearing a wedding veil." Biela snuck in, overflowing with tears and mischief.

Saul asked in his classiest store style, "Yes, Miss?"

She uttered in Yiddish, "I want a white lace wedding veil." Soul jerked when she spoke. The joke had run its course for Biela. She shrieked uncontrollably, her arms reaching out to touch him over the counter, "Srul, my dear Soul!"

He withdrew, turning pale and panting for air.

Leah rushed in and sobbed, "Ah, my lovely ones!" In the end, God has been gracious to you.

He shouted out, wondering, "But—but—how did you get in?".

Leah added, "Never mind how we got in," with every scar shining with tears and joy. "And where is Tsirrélé—my dear little Tsirrélé?"

She is out marketing with the mother, I hear.

The mother, too?

She is healthy and content.

Leah exclaimed, "Thank God! " and motioned for the porter carrying the bundles.

He flushed, "But—but I let the room." I was unaware of that and could not afford it.

"We'll find a room, so don't worry. The sun is still rising." Together, they agreed.

In the interim, Srul had started tinkering tensely with a pair of scissors. He tore a magnificent piece of fabric to pieces.

Biela finally said, "What are you doing?"

He laughed tensely and said, "Oh—I—." "So you did, after all, breach the barricade. We can't talk right now since I have customers every minute. Biela, go inside and take a nap; a sofa is in the parlor.

I want to speak with you, Leah.

Biela entered the parlor through the rear entrance, feeling a little chilly. Leah glanced at him as she did so.

Leah murmured hoarsely, "Something is wrong, Saul. Tsirrélé isn't present.

You feared telling us.

He lowered his head. I tried my hardest.

She is unwell, possibly even dead! My

His head sagged. "I gave it my all."

"She is sick—possibly even dead! My lovely angel!"

His eyes were now open. "Dead? No, I'm wed!"

"What! To who?"

He went sickeningly white. "To me."

Leah had never been so close to passing out during her lengthy search of the canopy. This was far worse than Ellis Island's nightmare. The scene recurred, and Tsirrélé's youthful beauty, untarnished by the journey, suddenly appeared before her. The "baby" had grown into a young woman of fifteen during those unrecognized years, while Biela was aging and stalling.

She mumbled, "But—but this will shatter Biela's heart," in a sad voice.

How could I have known Biela would ever enter? He attempted to sound enraged. "Was I to breach the Almighty's commandment and live as a bachelor my entire life? I waited patiently for Biela all those years—did I not?"

She said, "You could have migrated somewhere else."

"And break my connection—and go hungry?" By now, he was furious.

"In addition, I married into the family, so it is essentially the same.

The elderly mother shares the same joy."

"Oh, she!" The exclamation included all the bitterness that had been borne over the many years. She only desires grandkids.

No, he answered, it's not. grandkids with healthy eyes.

The lump in Leah's throat only permitted her to respond, "God forgives you." She tried to reclaim her soul for the benefit of Biela while steadying herself with a hand on the counter.

When a client entered, the terrible world became more prosaic and ribbons appeared in unappealing colors.

As Saul clanked the coins into the till, Leah replied, "Of course, we must leave this instant. Biela is no longer allowed to live with you here.

Sulkily, he agreed, "Yes, it is better that way. "And you might as well find out right away. Biela would not have liked the fact that I am open on the Sabbath. Another justification for not getting married to Biela is that. It doesn't appear to bother Tsirrélé."

The very ruins of her world appeared to be falling now. The second revelation of Tsirrélé's and his evil, though, seemed to fit in perfectly with the first and went a long way toward explaining it.

You do violate the Sabbath, after all.

His shoulders shook in response. "We have left Poland behind. No dead flies here. Everyone complies. Close the shop two days per week! I should proceed left.

And you carry your mother's grey hairs with you to the grave in grief.

"No longer is a foolish black 'Shaitel' covering my mother's grey hairs. Just that. I've told her that we live in a free and enlightened nation called America. Her eyes are now open.

"Your father's peace be upon him, I put my faith in God!

still exist

"A foolish black "Shantel" is no longer covering up my mother's grey hairs. That's it. She has heard me tell her that America is the home of freedom and wisdom. She opens her eyes."

"I put my faith in God—peace be with your father!

— remain closed! "Leah remarked as she took careful, deliberate steps inside the parlor to carry off her injured lamb.

Printed by Libri Plureos GmbH in Hamburg,
Germany

9 798887 830520